ITEMS SHOULD BE RETURNED
SHOWN BELOW. ITEMS NOT A
READERS MAY BE RENEWED B
WRITING, OR BY TELEPHONE. TO
AND THE NUMBER ON THE BARC

FINES CHARGED FO
POSTAGE INCURRE
OF ITEMS WILL BE

LEABHARLANN   D

Dublin City
Baile Átha Cliath

Date Due

14. DEC 04

2 2 FEB 201

10 DEC 20

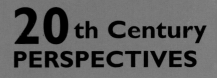

20th Century
PERSPECTIVES

The Causes of
World War I

Tony Allan

Heinemann
LIBRARY

H www.heinemann.co.uk
Visit our website to find out more information about Heinemann Library books.

To order:
☎ Phone 44 (0) 1865 888066
🖹 Send a fax to 44 (0) 1865 314091
🖥 Visit the Heinemann Bookshop at www.heinemann.co.uk to browse our catalogue
and order online.

First published in Great Britain by Heinemann Library,
Halley Court, Jordan Hill, Oxford OX2 8EJ,
a division of Reed Educational and Professional Publishing Ltd.
Heinemann is a registered trademark of Reed Educational and Professional Publishing Ltd.

OXFORD MELBOURNE AUCKLAND
JOHANNESBURG BLANTYRE GABORONE
IBADAN PORTSMOUTH (NH) USA CHICAGO

Produced for Heinemann Library by Discovery Books Limited
Designed by Ian Winton
Illustrated by Stefan Chabluk
Consultant: Stewart Ross
Picture research by Rachel Tisdale
Originated by Dot Gradations
Printed by Wing King Tong in Hong Kong

ISBN 0 431 12006 4
06 05 04 03 02
10 9 8 7 6 5 4 3 2 1

British Library Cataloguing in Publication Data
Allan, Tony, 1946 –
The causes of World War I. – (20th century perspectives)
1.World War, 1914-1918 – Causes – Juvenile literature
I.Title
940.3'11

Acknowledgements
The publishers would like to thank the following for permission to reproduce photographs:
Art Archive p. 39; Corbis p. 19; Mary Evans pp. 8, 9, 10, 12, 14, 16, 20, 24, 25, 26, 29, 30, 33, 38;
Hulton Archive pp. 34, 37, 42; Hulton Deutsch p.15; Hulton Getty pp. 4, 6, 17, 21, 32, 35, 43; David
King Collection p. 11; Peter Newark pp. 5, 13, 18, 22, 28, 31, 40; Popperfoto p. 27.

Cover photograph of Franz Ferdinand, Archduke of Austria and his wife reproduced with permission
of Hulton Archive.
Every effort has been made to contact copyright holders of any material reproduced in this book.
Any omissions will be rectified in subsequent printings if notice is given to the publishers.

Any words appearing in the text in bold, **like this**, are explained in the glossary.

Contents

What was World War One?

Saturday 1 July 1916 dawned sunny above the trenches. For many months, British and French forces had been confronting German troops, similarly dug in, across a ravaged wasteland a few hundred metres wide. Then at 7.30 a.m., the order came for the British troops to go 'over the top'. Their commanders had decided that the only way out of the bloody **stalemate** was an all-out assault. So the Battle of the Somme began.

Over the next four months, the war-torn meadows north of the River Somme in northern France were home to killing on a massive scale. Soldiers on both sides were **raked** by rifle and machine-gun fire as they surged across **no-man's-land**. By the end of October, when the battle finally drew to a close, British **casualties** amounted to 420,000, French to almost 200,000, and German to around 500,000 – a total of over a million men. In return for the sacrifice, the British and French forces had managed to win back about 10 kilometres (6 miles) of shattered wasteland.

Scottish troops go 'over the top', leaving the trenches to launch an attack on the German front line, during the Battle of the Somme.

Trench warfare
Much of the fighting in World War One took place in and between trenches – deep ditches protected by barbed wire. It was from these trenches that armies launched attacks on each other. Once soldiers left the relative safety of the trenches by going 'over the top', there was little to protect them from enemy fire. Soldiers defending their own trenches were often armed with machine guns that could fire hundreds of bullets every minute. Inevitably this led to many more of the attacking soldiers being killed than the soldiers defending the trenches.

The war that changed the world

The Battle of the Somme was only one of dozens of murderous confrontations in World War One. The war involved not just French, German and British forces but also, among others, Austrians, Hungarians, Russians, Italians, Turks, Australians, New Zealanders and Canadians. For the last nineteen months of the war the Americans also joined. Until then the USA had followed a policy of isolation as they wanted to keep out of any European conflict. The human cost of World War One, which finally came to an end in November 1918, was mind-boggling – about 10 million soldiers were killed with the greatest losses suffered by the Germans (1.8 million killed) and the Russians (1.7 million killed).

Russian forces wait for an attack on their trench on the Eastern Front in 1917. The wooden supports stopped the sides of the trench from collapsing.

Causes of catastrophe

The scale of the tragedy was so great that, even before the war was over, people on both sides were arguing fiercely over what could have caused the catastrophe. At the time they tended to blame their enemies. Eventually people on both sides came to realize that the roots of the conflict lay deep in the long-term rivalries of competing European countries. The system of **alliances** that bound different countries together and the general build-up of armies and weapons were also seen as possible causes. World War One may have broken out abruptly, but the causes of conflict had begun several decades earlier.

An English soldier writes home

English soldier Lieutenant Will Mulholland wrote a letter home describing what he saw on the Somme battlefront: 'Shall I tell you of the horrors – deaths in every form some calm and placid, some blasted and vaporized, some mutilated, one almost burnt to a cinder by me in a dugout?'

Background to the tragedy

At the start of the 20th century, Europe was easily the richest and most powerful region of the world. This was the time of **colonial** empires, when European countries ruled much of the globe. Europe owed its supremacy to the new wealth and progress created by the **Industrial Revolution**. Starting in Britain in the late 18th century, it had spread across the continent in the course of the 19th century, bringing new industries, fresh inventions and increased job opportunities. But the advance of industry had been patchy. Some countries, like Britain and Germany, had been in the forefront of economic progress. Others, like Russia, had lagged behind.

Rulers of the world

Above all Europe was self-confident. Its growing numbers of educated citizens believed they were living in the 'Age of Progress', a time when all problems could be solved by reason and clear thinking. As the pioneers of educated thought and economic development, Europeans believed that they had a duty to spread their civilization around the globe. That was their justification for colonial rule. Although it was already clear that some non-European powers – most notably the USA, but possibly also Japan – were catching up fast, many Europeans in 1900 truly believed that they ruled the world.

Tsar Nicholas II of Russia (left) shares a carriage with Kaiser Wilhelm II of Germany while on a state visit to Berlin in 1913. The two men were cousins by marriage. The kaiser was also closely related to King George V of Britain – they were both grandsons of Britain's Queen Victoria.

Few people at the time imagined that the engine of European civilization would shortly be derailed by a terrible war. Fewer still could have foreseen that such a disaster would be triggered by a single act of violence. Yet the event that set the world alight happened on 28 June 1914 in Sarajevo, the capital of Bosnia and Hercegovina, at the time a small province of the mighty Austro-Hungarian Empire.

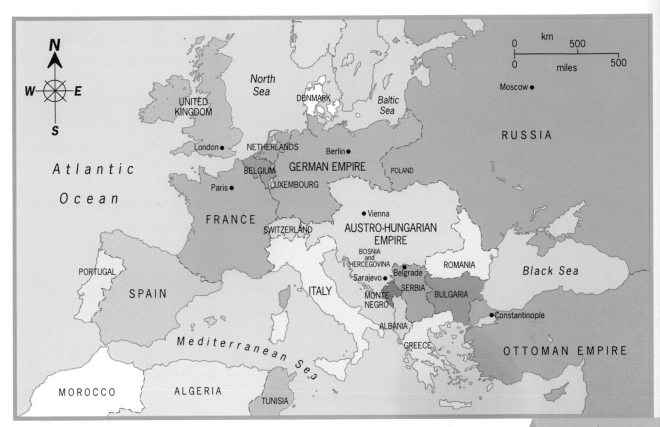

Descent into disaster

On that day Franz Ferdinand, the heir to the Austro-Hungarian throne, was **assassinated** by a terrorist during a ceremonial visit to the city. Blaming neighbouring Serbia for the attack, Austria-Hungary declared war. Serbia's **ally** Russia then came to its defence. When Russia started calling up its troops, Austria-Hungary's long-term ally and northern neighbour Germany believed itself also to be at risk. Fearing that it might be trapped in a war on two fronts, against both Russia and Russia's western ally, France, Germany's military leaders insisted on a lightning assault on France. This could only be achieved by striking through **neutral** Belgium. So, on 4 August 1914, German troops swept into Belgium. Britain then declared war on Germany in defence of Belgium. Just 37 days after the murder in Sarajevo, almost all Europe was at war, with France, Russia and Britain – called the 'Allies' – lined up against Germany and Austria-Hungary, called the **'Central Powers'**.

Events moved very quickly and even now historians argue about why the powers acted as they did. To make sense of what happened in those weeks it is necessary to look at each of the individual countries concerned and try to understand their particular ambitions, hopes and fears.

Austria-Hungary: the patchwork empire

The country that set the slide into war in motion was actually the least mighty of the great powers. Of the five leading countries that found themselves at war, Austria-Hungary had the smallest military budget and one of the smaller armies. Although it included areas of heavy industry, particularly around its twin capitals of Vienna and Budapest, much of its territory was still given over to agriculture.

Emperor Franz Josef was 84 years old when war broke out in 1914. He had been ruling Austria since 1848.

Austria-Hungary also faced difficult political problems. Its neighbour Germany was a newly established **nation-state** whose people shared the same language and history. By contrast the Austro-Hungarian Empire had been built up by its ruling family, the Habsburgs, who had held power in its Austrian heartland ever since the year 1282. Over the centuries they had built up their domains through war, marriage and **diplomacy**. As a result their people spoke many languages and had different customs and histories. There was in fact little to link all these many subjects other than their sometimes uncertain loyalty to the emperor.

Since 1848, that emperor had been Franz Josef, 84 years old when war broke out in 1914; Franz Ferdinand had been his nephew and heir.

The rising tide of nationalism

Because of the many different cultures within its borders Austria-Hungary was particularly at risk from the rising tide of **nationalism** that had swept across Europe in the course of the 19th century. In 1848, known throughout Europe as the 'Year of Revolutions', many of the peoples that made up the empire – Hungarians, Czechs, Croats and Romanians as well as Austrians – had risen up in revolt. The various uprisings had been put down bloodily, particularly the one in Hungary, which was only suppressed when Russia's **Tsar** Nicholas I sent a force of 200,000 men to his fellow-emperor's aid. Then from 1859 on, the Habsburgs' Italian lands had successfully broken away to join the independent kingdom of Italy.

From the 1870s onwards the emperor's main concern had been with the **Slav** peoples in the southern parts of the empire. For centuries the Slav lands had come under the control of the **Ottoman** Empire, ruled by **sultans** from Constantinople (now Istanbul in Turkey). The sultans' power had weakened during the 19th century, and so Austria-Hungary was able to take control of some formerly Ottoman lands. By 1900, Slavs made up nearly half the total population of Austria-Hungary, but many Slavs were unhappy with this situation and wanted to rule themselves.

Austria-Hungary's concerns over its Slav peoples grew towards the end of the 19th century with the appearance of a strong, independent Slav country on Austria-Hungary's southern borders. This was the kingdom of Serbia, which gained independence from Ottoman Turkey after the **Balkan** crisis of 1878. At first Serbia's rulers looked to Austria-Hungary for support, but the situation changed from 1903 on, when a new more nationalistic ruler took power. From then on, the Austro-Hungarian authorities were convinced that Serbs were working to undermine the loyalty of their own Slav subjects.

A magazine illustration of 1908 shows women in Serbian national dress learning to handle rifles. Serb nationalism was a powerful force in the years before World War One.

The 'sick man of Europe'

During the 17th century the Ottoman Empire, centred on Turkey, had covered large parts of eastern Europe and the Middle East. During the 19th century its power began to crumble and it became known as the 'sick man of Europe'. Some regions of the Ottoman Empire gained independence, like Greece, Serbia and Romania. Other parts of the empire were simply taken over by neighbouring states.

Russia: the slumbering giant

In 1905, Japanese forces celebrated a victory over Russia in the Far East in the Russo-Japanese War.

Like Austria-Hungary, Russia was an empire of many different races. Three centuries of expansion had stretched its borders from Germany in the west to the Pacific Ocean in the east. Physically, it was vast, covering one-seventh of the world's land area. More than half its land area was actually in Asia rather than Europe. As a result of its drive for conquest, less than half its peoples spoke Russian as their first language.

Everyone knew that, in the event of war, Russia would be a hard country to defeat. In the previous century the French leader Napoleon Bonaparte, having conquered all continental Europe, had come to grief when he invaded Russia. Even though he had captured Moscow (1811–12), the sheer size of the nation and its freezing winter weather had forced him to retreat, losing most of his men along the way.

The Russian steamroller

Russia's population was huge. By 1900 it had 130 million people – more than twice as many as Germany, and three times the populations of Britain or France. The peacetime strength of its army amounted to almost one and a half million men, while in war it could count on calling up another 5 million reservists (men who would be ready to become soldiers). The Russian army was nicknamed the 'steamroller' because it was seen to be slow to start but unstoppable once it got going. The belief that the Russian steamroller would eventually flatten all opposition was widespread across Europe, causing particular alarm in Austria-Hungary and Germany, its neighbours to the west.

Infinite resources

In respect for Russia's vast size, Britain's foreign minister, Sir Edward Grey, felt able to insist in a letter to France's president, Raymond Poincaré, shortly before World War One broke out that *'Russian resources are so great that in the long run Germany will be exhausted without our helping Russia.'*

Yet for all its huge size, Russia's army had not been particularly successful in military terms. In the 1850s, it had been defeated on its own territory by French and British forces in the **Crimean War**. A worse shock came in 1904–5, when Russia was defeated by the relatively small country of Japan in the Russo-Japanese War.

Shattered barricades litter a street in the Russian capital of St Petersburg during the 1905 uprising. The rioting broke out after Russia's shocking defeat by Japan.

Lagging behind

In fact there were many weaknesses in the Russian system. The **tsar** held absolute power over a land largely made up of **illiterate** peasants. Where other nations had brought in compulsory schooling and **democratic** reform, Russia had lagged behind. **Industrialization** had also started late in Russia. In 1900 the nation produced only one-tenth as much coal as Germany and one-fifth as much steel.

These weaknesses inevitably affected the nation's military strength. Armament factories could not produce enough weapons to keep the army adequately supplied and so it remained poorly equipped. The transport of troops was another problem. Russia had only a tenth of the railway lines per square kilometre of its territory as its western rivals. To add to these considerable problems the army was often poorly led by officers promoted for their social standing rather than their ability. Russia's minister for war, (1909-15) Vladimir Sukhomlinov, liked to boast, 'Look at me! I haven't read a military manual for the last 25 years.' Yet for all its weaknesses Russia remained a force feared by the rest of Europe.

Not enough weapons

When war broke out in 1914, Russia had only 60 artillery batteries (a group of guns used together), as compared with 381 in the German army, and each of its guns was supplied with only 850 shells, as opposed to more than 2000 for most other European armies.

Germany: insecure superpower

A painting of a German iron foundry dated 1900. Such industries helped to increase the wealth of the nation and made it possible for Germany to produce more weapons.

As a great power, Germany was a relative newcomer in 1914. It dated back only to 18 January 1871, when Wilhelm I had been crowned emperor of a newly-united land. Previously, the lands of German-speaking peoples had been a collection of **principalities** and minor kingdoms.

Germany's Iron Chancellor

The man who did most to unite Germany was the **aristocratic** politician Otto von Bismarck, who became known as the 'Iron Chancellor'. In 1862 he became prime minister of Prussia, the most powerful of the German states. Determined to create a united German realm under Prussian rule he fought three short, successful wars over the next nine years. The first was against Denmark, the second against Austria, and the third – the Franco-Prussian War of 1870-71 – against

France. It was after the Prussian victory over France that the new German Empire was proclaimed in 1871.

Having achieved his ambitions by war, Bismarck devoted his remaining nineteen years as head of a united Germany, to holding on to his gains by keeping the peace. He did so by maintaining a complicated series of **alliances**, designed above all to isolate France. France was still seething with resentment at its costly 1871 defeat. As the price of peace, it had to hand over to Germany the two provinces of Alsace and Lorraine together with a huge cash payment. In contrast, Bismarck mended relations with the Austrians. He created the League of the Three Emperors (1872), a friendly agreement between the emperors of Germany, Russia and Austria-Hungary. In 1879 Bismarck forged the more important Dual Alliance with Austria-Hungary. Three years later he persuaded Italy to join making it a **Triple Alliance**.

Bismarck's long hold on power in Germany finally came to an end in 1890, two years after the accession of a new emperor – in German called the 'kaiser'. Born with a withered left arm, Kaiser Wilhelm II combined moods of boundless ambition and self-confidence with periods of doubt. In Wilhelm's hands, German **diplomacy** suddenly changed direction, as we shall see.

The most dynamic country in Europe

The Germany that Wilhelm II inherited was the most dynamic country in Europe. Its industries were thriving, and its educational system was the best in the world. The nation's defence lay in the hands of a tightly-disciplined army that, when fully **mobilized**, was 2.2 million strong. Its military successes had encouraged fresh ambitions. Many Germans resented the fact that the unification of their country had come too late for them to build up a huge **colonial** empire like Britain's.

Kaiser Wilhelm II strikes a military pose in this portrait by P. A. Laszlo. His left arm, shown holding a sword, had in fact been withered from birth.

Bismarck's victories had also increased the army's already-high prestige. Prussia in particular remained a militaristic society, where pedestrians would step off the pavement if an army officer came by. Wilhelm's own love of everything military and his desire to extend Germany's empire led many in Europe to believe that he had ideas of world domination.

Blood and iron

Shortly after taking power as prime minister of Prussia, Bismarck gave a speech in which he said: 'Not by speeches and majorities will the great questions of the day be decided ... but by blood and iron.' This view was to have a lingering influence on German policy up to 1914.

France: wounded glory

France's fate in the 19th century was almost a reverse of Germany's. Where Germany found fresh prestige and strength, France suffered a decline in power and influence. The nation was used to glory. Under Louis XIV, the Sun King, France had dominated late 17th-century Europe, while in the 18th century the language of civilized people across the continent had been French. The French Revolution, which swept away the monarchy in 1789, was unable to provide a stable government. By the end of the century Napoleon Bonaparte had come to power and soon set about conquering Europe.

Political divisions

After Napoleon's final defeat in 1815 political instability again became a problem. In the course of the 19th century, France saw seven changes of regime, from republic to empire to monarchy and back to republic. In 1871, after their defeat in the Franco-Prussian War, the **Third Republic** was established. But even then there were constant changes of government. The nation had thirteen different foreign ministers in the nineteen years from 1871 to 1890. Nevertheless the nation bounced back from the disaster of the **Franco-Prussian War** surprisingly quickly. It managed to pay off the **war debt** to Germany within just three years. Yet the bitterness of the defeat remained, permanently souring relations between the two countries.

Following France's defeat in the Franco-Prussian War, Wilhelm I of Prussia is proclaimed emperor of a united Germany in the Hall of Mirrors at the Palace of Versailles. This palace, situated outside Paris, was once the home of French kings.

A gaping wound

The loss of Alsace and part of Lorraine to Germany after the Franco-Prussian War left France with an enduring sense of loss. Leon Gambetta, the statesman who did most to restore French fortunes after the defeat, once said, 'Never speak of it; think of it always.' France finally regained the lost provinces at the end of World War One.

A capital of culture

French citizens had much to be proud of during the Third Republic. Their culture still led Europe, thanks to the work of great writers like Victor Hugo, Gustave Flaubert, Emile Zola and Marcel Proust, musicians like Debussy and Ravel, and artists like Monet, Renoir, Cezanne and Gauguin. In addition France, and in particular its capital Paris, were famed around the world for their fashionable ways of life. In the USA people would joke, 'When good Americans die, they go to Paris.'

Economically the country made some progress, though it was still outpaced by its rival Germany. By 1914, France was producing only a third as much iron and steel as its bigger neighbour. More worrying still was the decline in its population. In 1870 the two countries had roughly the same number of people, but by 1914 France had around 38 million people compared to Germany's 65 million and Austria-Hungary's 52 million.

In this 1899 photograph, British and Egyptian flags fly at Fashoda in the Sudan, scene of a confrontation between French and British colonial forces the previous year.

A colonial power

Politically, France was still a world player. The country had a sizeable **colonial** empire, which by 1900 stretched over 10 million square kilometres (4 million square miles) of Africa, Indochina, the Caribbean and other parts of the world. It was second in size only to the British Empire. France's colonial ambitions at times brought her into conflict with Britain. In 1898 the two nations almost went to war over possession of the Sudan. This became known as the 'Fashoda Incident'. By 1904, however, Britain and France had settled their colonial differences as they both began to feel more threatened by Germany than they did by each other.

Britain: colonial flag bearer

As an island nation, Britain's outlook on the world was always different from that of its continental neighbours and rivals. Over a period of centuries, some of its most ambitious citizens had sought opportunities for trade and expansion overseas. The result was the British Empire, a gradual accumulation of **colonies** and **protectorates** that by the late 19th century stretched all around the globe and included Canada, southern Africa, Australia and India.

In many ways the empire was a source of strength for Britain. It provided **raw materials** for British industry and a market in which finished goods produced by British firms could be sold. Partly as a result of its pioneering role in the **Industrial Revolution**, Britain at the turn of the century was one of the wealthiest countries in the world producing as much iron as Germany and Austria-Hungary combined, and as much coal as all the major continental powers put together. However, both Germany and the USA were catching up fast, and in steel production as well as in newer technologies such as chemicals and electricity generation, Germany was already ahead.

Protecting the empire

The need to protect the colonies had shaped British **foreign policy** for much of the 19th century. The nation had fought a string of colonial wars, in Africa, India and the Far East. Britain also suspected Russia of having ambitions in central Asia and felt this might threaten its position in India.

Master of the seas

Of all the armed services, the navy was particularly important to Britain, for without it the empire could not survive. In the days before air travel, it alone could guarantee the passage of troops, administrators and trade goods to and from Britain. To ensure that 'Britannia ruled the waves', the

George V visits Bombay on a state visit to India in 1911. His royal titles included Emperor of India as well as King of Britain.

nation's military planners insisted in the 1890s that the British navy should be maintained to the 'two-power standard' – as large as any two other navies put together.

Concerned with protecting the empire, Britain's rulers were wary of continental involvements, seeing these as a diversion from the main goals of British policy. One government official even boasted of Britain's 'splendid isolation', unaffected by the **alliances** that bound the other European powers in an increasingly complicated web.

Yet Britain did have concerns about the political situation in Europe, and these had influenced its foreign policy for hundreds of years. This was a desire to maintain a **balance of power** in Europe so that no single nation would become strong enough to dominate all the others.

Jingoism

The term 'jingoism' comes from a song that was popular at the time of the **Balkan** conflict of 1878 (see page 9). It describes an attitude of blustering **patriotism**:

> 'We don't want to fight, but, by Jingo, if we do,
> We've got the ships, we've got the men, and got the money too.'

The USA: reluctant colossus

As the European powers competed for prestige and influence, one nation that kept itself apart was the USA. Separated from Europe by the 4500-kilometre (2813-mile) divide of the Atlantic Ocean, Americans for the most part considered themselves well rid of European squabbling. Many US citizens were recent immigrants or descendants of immigrants who had deliberately left the Old World to seek a fresh life in the USA and they were mostly glad to leave its problems behind them. American politicians liked to contrast the openness of America's **democratic**, **republican** society with Europe's social system where power was still based on **aristocratic** privilege.

A nation on the rise

Yet, whatever its wishes, the USA could not remain entirely unaffected by events in Europe and the rest of the world. The nation had undergone a remarkable change in the last four decades of the 19th century. Its population had soared, from 32 million in 1860 to 76 million in 1900 and was continuing to rise by more than 1 million every year, (in comparison Germany had 56 million people and Britain 41 million). The nation was also vastly wealthier, for **industrialization** had made it a world leader in economic terms, producing more coal than Germany and almost as much steel as Germany and Britain combined.

Inevitably, growing economic output meant more foreign trade, and trade in turn bound the USA to what was happening elsewhere in the world. Following the Spanish–American War of 1898, in which the republic easily defeated the forces of the old **colonial** power of Spain, the nation even acquired its first colonies, most notably the Philippine Islands in the Pacific. Like it or not, the USA had become a global power.

A painting showing Americans celebrating the official dedication of the Statue of Liberty in New York on 28 October 1886. The figure served as a beacon for generations of shipborne immigrants coming to the USA from Europe.

Italy opts out

The USA was not the only power to watch the events of August 1914 from the sidelines. Italy had been linked by treaty to the Central Powers since 1882. The **Triple Alliance** was, however, only defensive – Italy only had to support Germany if it was attacked and not if Germany itself was the attacker – a fact that the Italians would call on to avoid declaring war on the Allies in 1914. In fact Italy joined with the Allies in May 1915.

So when war finally broke out, it was impossible for the USA not to be affected. From the start, US citizens found themselves taking sides. There were 11 million Americans of German or Austro-Hungarian descent, and many of them passionately supported the **Central Powers**. Even so, public opinion generally backed the **Allies**, not least because so many other Americans traced their origins back to British ancestors. Economic ties with Britain and France also became important as the war drew on. US trade with these two countries increased dramatically between 1914 and 1916 due to the soaring demand for weapons.

The giant Carnegie steel works in Pennsylvania, USA, in 1905. The USA was the world's fastest-growing economic power in the years leading up to World War One.

Yet those considerations still lay ahead in 1914. At that time the USA was not in the mood for war. A popular song of the day was 'I Didn't Raise my Boy to be a Soldier.' Also no military preparations had been made. Although the navy was strong, the US army had only about 100,000 regular troops – a tiny force compared with the millions of men who had been called up in Europe.

American neutrality

On 18 August 1914, US President Woodrow Wilson spelled out to the American people his government's position on the war in Europe. Insisting that Americans should be '**neutral** in fact as well as in name, impartial in thought as well as in action ...'.

Shifting alliances

The **assassination** of Franz Ferdinand was the trigger for war in 1914, but one reason why a local conflict became a world war was the system of **alliances** linking or dividing the great powers. Treaty obligations required Germany to side with Austria–Hungary against Russia over the matter of war with Serbia. But, as we shall see, it wasn't the only reason Germany supported Austria–Hungary. Similarly, it wasn't just **diplomatic** links that led France to take Russia's side.

For centuries past European powers had relied on diplomacy to keep a **balance of power** that would ensure that no one nation could dominate all the others. As nations jostled to gain advantage over one another, the treaties that linked different countries together often included secret clauses. These stated what particular action each partner in the treaty would take in different crisis situations. This helped to create an atmosphere of international mistrust in which spying flourished. The sale of state secrets by disloyal officials also became a part of international relations.

Even though he left office in 1890, Germany's Iron Chancellor, Otto von Bismarck, did much to set up the system of alliances that prevailed in Europe up to World War One. This portrait was painted by Paul Reith in 1915.

The patterns of diplomacy are most easily understood when grouped into three broad phases. The first was the pattern set by Bismarck from 1871 to 1890. The second was the new course set by Kaiser Wilhelm II from 1890 onwards. The third was the change in British diplomatic policy that took place at the start of the 20th century.

Bismarck's diplomacy

In pursuit of his goal of keeping France isolated, Bismarck built up relations with Austria–Hungary. A formal alliance was struck in 1879, and it was joined three years later by Italy, creating the **Triple Alliance**. Equally important to Bismarck's plan was maintaining good relations with Russia. In 1873, Germany, Austria–Hungary and Russia were informally linked in the League of the Three Emperors, an arrangement that survived until 1887. It was then replaced by the secret **Reinsurance Treaty** between Germany and Russia, which guaranteed that the two countries wouldn't go to war with one another.

Kaiser Wilhelm's new course

German **foreign policy** changed when Kaiser Wilhelm II came to power in 1888. Eager to make his mark, the new ruler decided to adopt what became known as a 'new course' in foreign policy. Unhappy at this change in foreign policy Bismark resigned in 1890. Soon after, Wilhelm refused to renew the Reinsurance Treaty, despite persistent Russian attempts to keep it in force. The result was a diplomatic revolution. Within months Russia and France had entered negotiations with one another. By 1893 they were formally **allied**. To Bismarck's alarm, France was no longer isolated and, with hostile powers to east and west, Germany found itself faced with the prospect of someday having to fight a war on two fronts – against France in the west and Russia in the east.

Britain's diplomatic revolution

Britain began to look vulnerable once the Triple Alliance, linking Germany, Austria-Hungary and Italy, was in place. Furthermore Germany's acquisition of new **colonies** in China, West Samoa and parts of Africa, as well as its economic successes, soon put pressure on Britain to abandon its isolationist position. So

from 1900 onwards Britain increasingly became linked with other world powers as she searched around for allies. The first alliance was with Japan in 1902. Then, in 1904, came the **Entente Cordiale** – 'cordial understanding' – with France, which settled colonial disputes and marked a new warmth in relations between the two countries. In 1907 a similar agreement was reached with Russia. With Germany and Austria-Hungary on one side, France, Russia and Britain on the other, the pattern of the August 1914 crisis had fallen into place.

Britain's King Edward VII salutes the French flag during the 1903 state visit that paved the way for the Entente Cordiale, linking the two countries in friendship.

21

The Schlieffen plan

The **alliance** system meant that disputes between any two of the European powers ran the risk of developing into a Europe-wide confrontation. A crucial step making armed conflict even more likely came in 1905 when Germany secretly adopted a new military strategy. Known as the Schlieffen plan it was drawn up in response to the threat, opened up by the Franco–Russian alliance, that Germany might have to fight a war on two fronts.

Waging war on two fronts

The plan was named after Count Alfred von Schlieffen, chief of the German general staff (supreme military commander) from 1891 to 1905. As early as 1892 he realized that Germany might have to divide its military forces in the event of a war. One army would be needed to fight the Russians on the nation's eastern border, another to fight the French in the west. The obvious danger was that Germany's forces, split two ways, would be crushed like a nut in a nutcracker.

Russian troops on parade in 1914. German fears of Russian military strength lay behind the formulation of the Schlieffen plan. The plan was designed to avoid the risk of Germany fighting a war on two fronts.

Von Schlieffen's solution was based on the idea that attack is often the best form of defence. He knew that Russia, because of its size and inefficient transport system, would be slow to **mobilize** in the event of war. The best estimates suggested that the process would take at least six weeks. The Schlieffen plan proposed that German forces should take advantage of this delay to deliver a knockout blow to France, the enemy in the west. Then, with France defeated, Germany would be free to concentrate all its armies on the Eastern Front, where they could use their combined might to bring the Russian steamroller to a halt.

However, France had used the years since the Franco-Prussian War to build strong defences along its border with Germany. A chain of fortresses all the way from Luxembourg to Switzerland were built to prevent just such an attack. To overcome this problem the Schlieffen plan proposed bypassing this frontier altogether. Instead, German forces would invade France through Belgium, choosing to attack the country's northern frontier. The plan, was very specific as to which targets should be reached and taken for each day that it was in operation. The invading army had to keep to a strict timetable if France was to be defeated within the required six weeks.

An act of aggression

One problem with the plan was that since 1839 Belgium had been a **neutral** country, with its neutrality guaranteed by all the major European powers, including Germany. Invading Belgium would therefore be an obvious act of aggression. Yet the plan's authors were unfazed by this detail. Von Schlieffen and his successors assumed, it seems, that Belgium would let the German troops pass through without a fight.

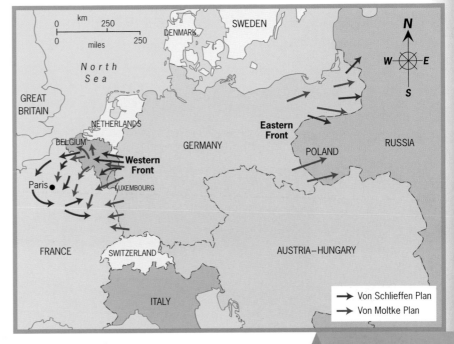

This map shows the planned areas of attack on the Eastern and Western fronts as described in the Schlieffen plan. By the time the plan was finally put into action in 1914, changes had been made by the German commander-in-chief, Helmut von Moltke.

When the plan was finally put into action in 1914, the Belgians chose instead to resist. The German invasion along with the attacks on ordinary Belgian civilians profoundly shocked neutral opinion. It was Germany's invasion of Belgium that finally united Britain on the need to go to war. The aggression also did much to turn public opinion in the USA against the **Central Powers**, and so helped to ensure that when America did join the conflict, it was on the **Allied** side.

The gist of the plan

General von Schlieffen explained the logic that lay behind his strategy: 'Germany must strive ... first to strike down one of the allies while the other is kept occupied; but then, when the one antagonist is conquered, it must, by exploiting its railways, bring a superiority of numbers to the other **theatre of war**, which will also destroy the other enemy.'

Flashpoints overseas: the colonies

When countries linked themselves together through formal and informal **alliances** they did so because they believed this would prevent war. But the alliance system could not stop the competition and **colonial** rivalry that continued to provide an opportunity for conflict in the overseas colonies. Wilhelm II's determination to get involved in colonial affairs only added to this problem. The **Boer War**, which took place in South Africa (1899–1902) between British settlers and the 'Boers' (a name given to the early Dutch and German settlers) was one such colonial conflict. Germany's support for Britain's Boer opponents played a part in souring relations between the two countries and pushing Britain into an alliance with Russia and France.

*The Italian flag is raised over Tripoli, capital of Libya, in 1911. Italy's success in taking Libya from the Ottomans encouraged the **Balkan** countries to declare war on Turkey the following year.*

Targeting North Africa

As the new century got under way, the focus of colonial expansion turned towards North Africa. This was one of the few parts of the continent that had not already been extensively colonized. The region also had great strategic importance because it was so close to Europe.

The main colonial power in the area in 1900 was France, which had ruled Algeria since 1830, and had strong influence in neighbouring Tunisia. The British had a presence there, having established a **protectorate** over Egypt in 1882. Italy also had ambitions in the region. Seeking belatedly to build up an empire of its own, it set its sights on Libya, which it finally snatched from **Ottoman** control in 1911.

Crisis in Morocco

One of the few countries in North Africa to successfully maintain its independence was Morocco. Throughout the 19th century it had been ruled by native **sultans**. But it became vulnerable after 1894, when the crown passed into the hands of a thirteen-year-old boy.

In 1905, Wilhelm II chose to make a highly publicized visit to the sultan in Tangier during which he offered the sultan German support for Moroccan independence. This was seen as a direct challenge to France. From their base in neighbouring Algeria, the French had taken it for granted that the weakened nation should naturally fall under their **sphere of influence**. In 1906, to resolve this **diplomatic** crisis, the Algeciras Conference was convened. Britain, seeing Germany as its main rival, decided to stand by the **Entente Cordial** and back France. Germany was forced to accept the agreements made at the conference.

A more serious crisis blew up in 1911 when French troops broke the Algeciras agreement. Germany, feeling dissatisfied with its diplomatic efforts in the 1905–6 crisis took a more aggressive approach by sending a gunboat, the *Panther*, to the Moroccan port of Agadir. The act was seen as a direct challenge to France, and for a time the possibility of war loomed large. Britain, declaring it would support France against Germany, put the British naval fleet on alert. Once again the Germans had to back down. In the negotiations that followed, France agreed to buy off German claims to Morocco by handing over some colonial territories further south in Africa, in the Congo basin.

The two Moroccan crises were both settled peacefully. It looked as if the alliance system was working. But as Britain and Russia had on both occasions supported France it was beginning to look to Germans as if their country was in danger of being encircled by a ring of hostile powers.

Kaiser Wilhelm II's official visit to Morocco in 1905 set off an international crisis, as France and its ally Britain regarded the country as falling within the French sphere of influence.

The arms race

The introduction of HMS Dreadnought in 1906 launched a new era in naval ship-building. The ship's high speed and the range of its huge guns made all other battleships obsolete.

In the decade leading up to the war there was increasing competition between the European powers to match or outdo one another in military might. The spiralling spending on weapons in fact turned out to be self-defeating. As one country built up its army, another would feel the need to do the same. With larger armies and more weapons the prospect of war in Europe became more likely.

Building more battleships

When Germany decided to build up its own navy (it passed naval laws in 1898 and 1900), it was Britain who felt most threatened. As the largest **colonial** power Britain felt it had to maintain its mastery of the seas. At first Britain felt that its naval superiority was so great that there was little prospect of the Germans catching up. The British, however, increased

the pace of the naval race in 1906 when they introduced a new battleship, called HMS ***Dreadnought***. The Dreadnought's size and speed, and its battery of big guns, which could fire further than those of any previous warship, made all existing battleships obsolete (no longer of any use).

Germany announced that it would build four of the new Dreadnoughts. Suddenly Germany and Britain found themselves in serious competition. By 1910 Britain had, at great expense, established a clear lead in this class of ship, building eleven Dreadnoughts to Germany's eight. In 1912 Germany turned its attention to expanding its army.

Call to arms

Germany began building up its army because it realized that the forces of the **Central Powers** were heavily outnumbered by those of Russia and France. Together, the standing armies of Germany and Austria-Hungary numbered roughly a million men, while those of their two potential enemies reached nearly twice that figure. Part of the reason for the limited size of the German army was political. Germany's **aristocratic** officer corps (special group) had traditionally resisted any sizeable increase that would have opened up their ranks to the despised middle classes. Now, however, necessity demanded change,

and the German parliament passed a measure designed to boost recruitment immediately by some 60 per cent. France responded by increasing its period of **conscription** (compulsory military service) from two to three years, while Russia announced a 'Great Programme' designed to enlarge its army by 40 per cent over the next three years.

Prussian guards goose-step on parade before Kaiser Wilhelm II. By 1914 Germany feared that its army was outnumbered by those of its rivals to the east and west.

Even more alarmingly from the German point of view, the French agreed to loan money to the Russian government that would enable it to build an extra 5000 kilometres (3125 miles) of strategic railway by 1918. The entire Schlieffen plan rested on Russia's being slow to call up its troops, and that situation seemed about to change.

By mid-1914 Germany felt itself seriously under threat. The military balance seemed to be swinging against the Central Powers. From Germany's viewpoint if war had to come, it was better for Germany that it should come soon.

The hammer or the anvil

Germany's chancellor, Prince Bernhard von Bulow, put the case for expanding the armed forces in a speech he gave in 1899: *'The means of fighting the battle for existence in this world without strong armaments on land and water, for a nation soon to count 60 millions, living in the centre of Europe and at the same time stretching out its economic feelers in all directions, have not yet been found. In the coming century the German nation will either be the hammer or the anvil.'*

The Balkan cauldron

Many years before the outbreak of war in 1914, Germany's Iron Chancellor Otto von Bismarck had predicted that 'some foolish thing in the **Balkans'** would provide the spark to set all Europe ablaze. Events would prove him right.

The Balkan region of eastern Europe was made up of many different peoples including Greeks, Macedonians, Albanians, Serbs, Croats, Bosnians, Bulgarians and Romanians. The instability of the Balkan region stemmed from the declining power of the **Ottoman** Turks. Austria-Hungary and Russia both wished to take over its European possessions. But the **Slav** peoples of this region, spearheaded by the independent Slav kingdom of Serbia, wanted to rule themselves, free of the control of any **imperial** power. Although Russia had traditionally supported the Slavs cause, an agreement with Austria-Hungary in 1897 and 1903 had kept the peace in the region for a decade.

Crisis over Bosnia

This changed in 1908 when Austria-Hungary's foreign minister, Count Aehrenthal, decided to **annex** the Slav territory of Bosnia and Hercegovina into the empire. Russia secretly agreed to the move because Austria-Hungary promised to support it on naval issues. In fact Russia never got its side of the deal – it had hoped to gain access for Russian warships, through the Dardanelles Straits, to the Mediterranean Sea. Russia's **ally** Serbia was outraged as it had hoped to take over the territories itself. As a result, Russia emerged from the situation with its reputation as a champion of the Slav cause badly damaged.

28

In 1912, full-scale war broke out in the Balkan region. The trigger was Italy's seizure of Libya from Turkey in the previous year, which had shown just how weak the Ottoman regime had become. In response, Serbia, allied with Greece and Bulgaria, seized control of Ottoman Turkey's Macedonian lands. The allies rapidly achieved total victory, winning almost all the Ottoman's remaining territories in Europe. They then fell out over the division of the spoils, and a second Balkan War was fought in 1913, this time between Bulgaria on the one hand and its two former allies on the other. Bulgaria lost, and was forced to hand over many of the gains it had made the previous year.

Serbia victorious

The chief winner from the two wars turned out to be Serbia, which nearly doubled in size. Austria-Hungary watched the Serbs' success with mounting alarm. In the peace conference held in London in May 1913 that brought the first Balkan war to an end, Austria-Hungary used its influence to ensure that Serbia should not get access to the sea, as it wished. Instead, the independent kingdom of Albania was created, stretching along the Adriatic coastline. Once more Russia took no action to defend Serbian interests in the face of Austro-Hungarian pressure.

The Balkan Wars set the scene for the tragedy at Sarajevo. In the wake of the Serb advance in 1912, Austria-Hungary had initially wanted to send its army to intervene, and had only been persuaded to hold back when its ally Germany refused to lend its support. In 1914 Austria-Hungary was still spoiling for a fight with its smaller southern neighbour. Russia, however, was smarting from what it regarded as two successive **diplomatic** defeats. Neither power was in a mood to compromise, as the events following the **assassination** of Franz Ferdinand would show.

Macedonian civilians drive out occupying Bulgarian troops following the second Balkan War as shown in this newspaper illustration from 1913. In this conflict, Bulgaria lost most of the gains it had made in the previous year.

The road to war

A magazine illustration reconstructs the moment when a Serbian nationalist shot Archduke Franz Ferdinand and his wife in Sarajevo on 28 June 1914. This assassination set in motion the events that led to the outbreak of war.

On the morning of 28 June 1914 Franz Ferdinand and his wife arrived in Sarajevo. A first attempt to **assassinate** the archduke was made when a bomb was thrown into his car as it drove towards the town hall. Quick thinking by the archduke, who managed to throw the bomb away, saved their lives – but only for a short time. When the driver of their car took a wrong turning he inadvertently drove them into the path of another assassin who, seizing this unexpected opportunity, took out his gun and shot both the archduke and his wife dead.

Death in Sarajevo

One of the individuals in the plot to assassinate Archduke Franz Ferdinand described the murder: 'As the car came abreast he [assassin Gavrilo Princip] stepped forward from the curb, drew his automatic pistol from his coat and fired two shots. The first struck the wife of the archduke, the Archduchess Sofia, in the abdomen. She was an expectant mother. She died instantly. The second bullet struck the archduke close to the heart. He uttered only one word, "Sofia!" – a call to his stricken wife. Then his head fell back and he collapsed.'

It is clear now that the events in Sarajevo triggered the outbreak of the war, but at the time few people guessed that anything so terrible was about to happen. Sadly, political assassinations were only too common at the time. Russia alone had lost a **tsar**, a prime minister, and dozens of other dignitaries to the bomb or the bullet over the previous 35 years. After the killing of Franz Ferdinand, most people, however shocked, expected Austria-Hungary to come to terms with the loss. Few European political leaders bothered to cancel their summer holidays in expectation of serious trouble.

This time, however, Austria-Hungary was determined to make an example of the Serbs. Knowing that several would-be assassins had been in Sarajevo on the fateful day the Austro-Hungarian government immediately decided that the assassination had been organized in Serbia. Now the authorities decided that the killing provided an ideal opportunity for crushing Serbia once and for all.

The kaiser's blank cheque

Before taking action, Austria-Hungary needed to get the support of their powerful German **ally**. On 5 July 1914 Kaiser Wilhelm responded positively with a 'blank cheque' of support. This blank cheque, so-called because it allowed Austria-Hungary to do whatever it wanted, marked the next step on the road to war.

The reasons for Germany's decision in 1914 went well beyond the natural sympathy felt by the kaiser over the death of a fellow royal. It was also shaped by the belief that Austria-Hungary must be seen to take firm action if the nation was to keep its standing among the great powers. Germany also expected that because Russia was fiercely anti-terrorist it would sympathize more with Austria-Hungary than with Serbia. Not expecting war, the kaiser happily set off next day on a three-week sea cruise in the Baltic.

A nation ready for war

There were other considerations underlying the German decision to support Austria-Hungary. The nation had been working for the past eight years to widen the Kiel Canal, linking the Baltic and the North Seas, so **Dreadnought**-sized battleships could pass through it without going around Denmark. That work had just been completed. Germany's military planners knew that, if war should come, their position against France and Britain was as good as it was ever likely to be. Germany's commander-in-chief, Helmut von Moltke had recently told his Austrian counterpart, 'We are ready, and the sooner the better for us.' Germany's leaders may not have expected a European war when they issued the blank cheque, but they were well prepared for it should it come.

Kaiser Wilhelm (centre) attends military manoeuvres with his commander-in-chief, Helmut von Moltke, early in 1914. When the time came it was von Moltke who was responsible for putting the Schlieffen plan into action.

31

Ultimatum to Serbia

For 25 days after the killing in Sarajevo, nothing publicly seemed to happen, although frenzied **diplomatic** activity was in fact under way in Vienna the capital of Austria. Then, on 23 July, Austria-Hungary delivered its **ultimatum** – a list of demands to Serbia. The Austro-Hungarians had delayed sending the ultimatum partly because the government was not at first united on the right course to take. Also they wanted the nation's farmers to have time to bring in the harvest before possibly being called up to serve in a war. When the message was finally sent, however, it was expressed in such strong language as to make war almost inevitable. The Serbs were asked not just to crack down on all organizations considered hostile to Austria-Hungary and to arrest those involved with them, but also to allow Austro-Hungarian police and military into Serbia to help hunt them down. Serbia was given just two days to accept the terms or face war. Eager to avoid that risk, the Serbs in fact indicated that they were prepared to consider all the demands except the presence of Austro-Hungarian police on their territory. Seizing upon that refusal, the authorities in Vienna at once rejected the reply.

Austria-Hungary declares war

Suddenly all Europe realized the seriousness of the crisis. Yet on 26 July a general war still seemed a long way off. Similar confrontations had in the past been settled by diplomacy, and now Sir Edward Grey, the British foreign minister, proposed a conference of all the powers at which the issues could be sorted out. This time, however, Austria-Hungary was in no mood to settle the crisis through debate with other countries. Germany backed its stand, and on 28 July Austria-Hungary formally declared war on Serbia. The Serb capital of Belgrade was bombarded the following day.

German officer cadets receive a lecture on aeroplane engines in early 1914. World War One was the first conflict in which aviation played a significant part.

Gauging the Russian reaction

All eyes now turned to St Petersburg to see Russia's reaction. Would the **tsar's** government stand by while its Serb **ally** was attacked, or would it send troops to intervene? There were strong arguments against getting involved. The 'Great Programme' to expand the army had barely got under way. Also previous wars had not gone well for Russia and had led to popular outcries against the tsar's rule. Encouraged by assurances of French support, the tsar did not hesitate for long. On 29 July he gave orders for Russian forces to **mobilize** against Austria–Hungary. A confrontation between two of the great powers now seemed inevitable, but hope remained that it could still be limited to Austria–Hungary and Russia. Frantic diplomatic efforts continued to prevent the other powers from becoming involved.

On 2 August 1914, crowds gather in Berlin to listen to an officer announcing that Germany had declared war on Russia.

COUNTDOWN TO WAR

THE KEY DATES OF THE 1914 CRISIS WERE:

28 JUNE — ASSASSINATION OF FRANZ FERDINAND IN SARAJEVO
5 JULY — KAISER WILHELM GIVES THE 'BLANK CHEQUE' TO AUSTRIA-HUNGARY
23 JULY — AUSTRO-HUNGARIAN ULTIMATUM TO SERBIA
28 JULY — AUSTRIA-HUNGARY DECLARES WAR ON SERBIA
30 JULY — RUSSIA ORDERS GENERAL MOBILIZATION
1 AUGUST — GERMANY DECLARES WAR ON RUSSIA
3 AUGUST — GERMANY DECLARES WAR ON FRANCE
3 AUGUST — GERMAN TROOPS INVADE BELGIUM
4 AUGUST — BRITAIN DECLARES WAR ON GERMANY

Timetables to war

In the end some of the key decisions that turned a local war in Serbia into a European war revolved around the most unlikely factor: railway transport. The reasons were connected with military planning in Russia, Germany and France. In each of these countries, generals were convinced of the vital importance of speed in responding to any military threat. At a time when motor transport was still a novelty, moving armies rapidly meant putting them on trains. Stressing the need for mobility, a German military maxim of the late 19th century was, 'Build no more fortresses; build railways'. When **Tsar** Nicholas II gave the order for Russian armies to be called up, something like panic spread through Europe's foreign ministries. In Germany, Wilhelm II was particularly alarmed as he had expected Russia to stand down.

All or nothing for Russia

The main focus of concern for Kaiser Wilhelm was Nicholas II, his distant cousin. He implored the tsar to stop Russian **mobilization**, promising in exchange to put pressure on Austria-Hungary to negotiate over Serbia. For a moment it seemed that his **diplomacy** might work. In response Nicholas gave orders that Russian troops should be called up only on the Austro-Hungarian border, not the German one as well. Within hours, though, the order was changed. Nicholas had learned from his generals that Russia's military planning simply did not allow for a limited mobilization. It had to be all or nothing if the call-up was not to collapse into chaos.

Crowds gather in the rain to watch German troops as they march into the Belgian capital city of Brussels in August 1914. Resistance to the German invasion led to many Belgian civilians being killed.

In Germany railway schedules were also an important military concern. The entire Schlieffen plan depended on getting the right troops to the right place at the right time. General mobilization involved no fewer than 11,000 trains, all of them travelling to an exact timetable. So Wilhelm tried to limit the conflict by asking for troops to be called only to the

Russian front to avert the risk of war with France. But he too was informed that it could not be done. A general war, it seemed, could not be avoided as years of military planning had made it inevitable.

Would Britain fight?

The final uncertainties concerned Britain and Italy. Italy had been part of the **Triple Alliance** with Germany and Austria–Hungary since 1879, but only for

purposes of defence. As for Britain, the nation was linked to France and Russia by two separate **ententes**, but had no firm treaty obligations forcing it to fight. Although Sir Edward Grey himself thought war must come, a majority of the British **cabinet** were against getting involved in a continental conflict.

What swung the balance in Britain was the question of the rights and wrongs of the situation. It soon became apparent that the British government would only unite in favour of war in the case of obvious, unprovoked aggression. Realizing the importance of the issue, the French government pulled its troops 10 kilometres (6 miles) back from the German border to prevent any suggestion that France had started the fighting.

It took the German invasion of **neutral** Belgium on 3 August, as part of the Schlieffen plan, to finally turn the tide of British public opinion. Germany had already declared war on Russia and France, and now Britain declared war on Germany. That same day, Italy announced that it would remain neutral. At this stage only Germany, Russia, France, Austria–Hungary and Britain were at war. But soldiers from the British and French empires would soon be shipped to Europe to take part in the fighting. In the months and years to come other nations would be drawn into the conflict.

In World War One trains were an important way of moving troops to the front line. In this picture the troops on the train are Serbian. To begin with the Serbs had some successes against Austro-Hungarian forces, but they were finally crushed by a joint German–Austrian campaign late in 1915.

Why did the war last so long?

Most of the decision-makers in August 1914 expected a short, sharp war. British troops went to war expecting to be home by Christmas, while the kaiser, going one step further, told troops leaving for the front in August that they would be back 'before the leaves have fallen from the trees'.

The collapse of the Schlieffen plan

The war would indeed have been short if the Schlieffen plan had worked, but it did not. Belgian resistance slowed down the initial assault. Then Russia surprised the military planners by invading eastern Germany earlier than expected so that troops had to be diverted east to meet the threat. In a decisive battle, the French held the German forces at the River Marne, north-east of Paris, and on 10 September, one day short of the six weeks allowed for the capture of Paris, von Moltke actually had to order a limited German retreat.

The two sides then competed in a desperate race west – the so-called 'Race to the Sea'. By October, both sides on the Western Front were dug in behind continuous lines of fortifications that stretched 800 kilometres (500 miles) from the Swiss border to the English Channel.

The battlefronts of central Europe during World War One.

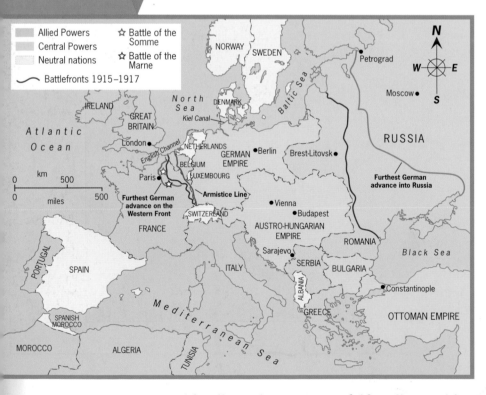

A blood-soaked balance of power

Ironically, once the trenches had been dug, the very **balance of power** that had been meant to guarantee peace came into play to ensure a long war. The rival **alliances** roughly balanced out, preventing either side from winning a decisive advantage. On paper, the **Allies** had greater reserves of manpower – over the course of the war they would call on the services of 40 million soldiers, while the **Central Powers** called up 25 million. In the early years, however, this surplus was more than countered by the strategic benefits of Germany's central position, which meant it could move troops efficiently between fronts as they were needed to meet fresh challenges.

The Germans' early victories in the west also meant that they simply had to hold onto their gains, while the burden of driving them back fell on the Allies. In the conditions of warfare at the time, attack was more costly than defence. A grim arithmetic calculated that men who went 'over the top', armed with rifles and bayonets to attack soldiers, with machine guns and dug into trenches, regularly suffered at least a third more **casualties** than the defenders.

War on the Eastern Front

On the Eastern Front the fighting was less bogged down than in the west. There the early Russian advances were soon reversed, and German troops advanced far into Russian Poland and even Russia itself. There were, however, still long periods of **stalemate** on both fronts and with neither side willing to back down, the war became a gaping hole swallowing up first thousands, then millions of corpses.

This staged photograph illustrates the benefits of wearing masks to combat the poison gas used as a weapon on the Western Front from 1915 on.

New weapons

In 1915 the Germans shocked world opinion by turning to chemical warfare in the form of **poison gas**. The following year saw the first tanks in action – they were used to lead attacks on the trenches. Probably the most important development in warfare was air power – once bombs could be dropped from the air, civilians as well as soldiers found themselves caught up in the conflict.

The US tips the balance

Throughout 1915 and 1916, the generals tried everything in their power to break the military **stalemate**. Both sides repeatedly sought and failed to smash through enemy lines with all-out assaults. The result was bloodbaths like the Battle of the Somme. At sea, the British imposed a naval **blockade** on the **Central Powers** that prevented vital supplies from getting through.

Each side also looked for new **allies**. Japan joined the Allied side in August 1914, while Ottoman Turkey came to the aid of the Central Powers two months later. Lured by the promise of big gains in North Africa and elsewhere, Italy finally entered the war in May 1915, on the Allied side. In the same year Bulgaria cast in its lot with Germany and Austria-Hungary. The war was gradually spreading beyond Europe. By far the most important new entrant, though, was the USA, which in April 1917 entered the war on the Allied side. Woodrow Wilson had long resisted getting involved, having fought and won the 1916 presidential election with the promise of keeping the USA out of the war.

Crowds gather in London to welcome the arrival of US troops in 1917. By mid-1918, a quarter of a million American soldiers were crossing the Atlantic each month.

The submarine menace

One reason for the USA entering the conflict was Germany's use of submarine warfare. In an attempt to counter the British naval blockade, military leaders had authorized the use of the newly invented **U-boats** against unarmed Allied **merchant ships**. Any ship suspected of trading with the Allies could be sunk without warning. Some of the civilian **casualties** that resulted were US citizens – notably 128 of the 1195 passengers and crew on board the British liner *Lusitania*, sunk in May 1915. German planners realized that the move would almost certainly bring the USA into the war. However, they also believed that if they could starve Britain out, by preventing food supplies from reaching British ports, this would outweigh the risk of US intervention.

Another incident that pushed the US to declare war was the Zimmerman telegram. Arthur Zimmerman, Germany's foreign minister, sent a coded message to a German diplomat in Mexico. The message suggested that if Mexico joined the Central Powers they would be given territory in the USA. The British secret service intercepted the message and eagerly passed it on to the US authorities.

When it finally came, the US declaration of war had little immediate impact, for there were few US troops ready to enter the combat. In the summer of 1917 a more important development was Britain's use of **convoys** of armed escorts for merchant ships, which counteracted the U-boat threat.

A German poster illustrates the effectiveness of U-boats (submarines) in sinking Allied shipping. Attacks on merchant ships helped bring the USA into the war. The German text reads 'Forward the U-Boats!'

Germany's last push for victory

Even so, late 1917 and early 1918 saw Germany come closer to outright victory than at any time since the start of the conflict. In 1917 the unstable Russian monarchy fell and within months a **communist** government took over. The nation's new leaders agreed to sign a peace treaty at Brest-Litovsk, in Poland, that gave Germany large areas of Russian land. Encouraged by this success, the German high command determined to use their last reserves to push for final victory in the west. In spring and summer 1918 they almost succeeded, advancing to within 60 kilometres (38 miles) of Paris.

But the vital breakthrough failed to come. The Allied line held, and the German army had nothing left to throw at it. At this point US reinforcements – there were nearly 2 million US troops in Europe by the end of the war – proved decisive. The Allies launched a series of counterattacks that forced the Germans back. By the end of August they had lost all their earlier gains and were still retreating.

The peace that never was

The war was by now turning against the **Central Powers** in other areas. Bulgaria surrendered to the **Allies** in September, soon followed by Ottoman Turkey and Austria-Hungary. With the Western Front buckling under Allied pressure, the German authorities realized that the game was up. On 8 November, Germany requested an **armistice**. On the 9 November Kaiser Wilhelm abdicated (gave up the throne). Two days later the guns finally fell silent. World War One was over.

Though a wave of relief greeted the end of the fighting, rejoicing was limited, even on the winning side. Too many people had died to make for easy celebrations. Besides, an economic downturn caused by the sudden closing of war industries and a worldwide flu epidemic, that killed almost as many people as the war itself, further dampened the mood.

The Fourteen Points

There was general agreement that the world had changed. People everywhere spoke of the conflict as the 'war to end war'. Yet few had any clear idea of what the new world order would look like. One person who did was Woodrow Wilson, who had outlined his proposals for peace to the US Congress in January 1918. The 'Fourteen Points' he put forward sketched a future based on **democracy** and the right of small nations to determine their own destiny. Blaming Europe's secret treaties, at least in part, for the outbreak of war, he also insisted on open **diplomacy**, along with **free trade** and steps towards **disarmament**.

It was a far-sighted programme, but in 1918 it fell largely on deaf ears. To war-weary European statesmen, the 'war to end war' meant crushing their enemies so they couldn't threaten European peace again.

Making Germany pay

In 1918, with millions of deaths to justify, victorious France and Britain hardly felt generous. Britain's prime minister, David Lloyd-George won re-election that year on a policy of 'making Germany pay'. France's premier Georges Clemenceau was understandably obsessed

A painting by Sir William Orpen shows ministers gathered to sign the Treaty of Versailles in June 1919. The setting was the Hall of Mirrors, where the German Empire had been declared in 1871.

with the danger a revived Germany might pose, and demanded severe restrictions on Germany's military strength as well as a zone along the border with France – the Rhineland – where all military installations would be banned. When the USA refused to cancel Allied **war debts**, he also demanded '**reparations**' from Germany to pay for the cost of the war.

The Treaty of Versailles signed in 1919 in many ways delivered the worst of all worlds. German public opinion was outraged. People who had been expecting victory just three months earlier and who had thought they were negotiating from a strong position now felt betrayed.

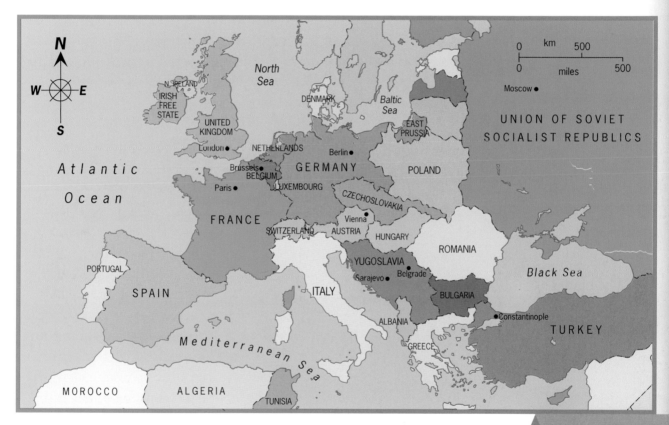

The countries of Europe between World War One and World War Two.

Germany was weakened by the settlement, which returned Alsace and Lorraine to France as well as some eastern territories to a newly independent Poland. But it was not fatally wounded. With the dissolution of the Austro-Hungarian and **Ottoman** Empires to its east and south which also followed on from the war, its strategic position was in many ways stronger. Alarmingly for France, the prestige of the German military was still as high as ever.

Not only did Germany now have grounds for seeking revenge but it was also in a stronger position to do so. Far from putting an end to war, the Versailles settlement had actually paved the way for the rise of Hitler and **Nazism**, and for the outbreak of a second world war just twenty years later.

Learning the lessons

The world that emerged from World War One was very different from that of 1914. The great European empires had gone for ever with the overthrow of the **tsar** in Russia and the collapse of Austria–Hungary. Germany also had lost its kaiser and had been reborn, for a time, as a **democratic republic**.

The victorious powers had changed too, even if the alterations were not quite so obvious. To start with, most of the **allies** were poorer. The war had been hugely costly and to pay the bills, both France and Britain had borrowed heavily. There had been social changes too. Women had taken over men's jobs when the men had been called up to fight, and their economic status had risen accordingly. Women's efforts during the war also went some way towards gaining them the vote in some countries. **Labour unions** had increased their influence, having been treated as partners by governments to boost the war effort.

A discharged soldier begs for money on the street in London in the 1920s. Across Europe, the war left many social problems in its wake.

Building a new world order

Some first steps were taken in the direction of Woodrow Wilson's new world order. The League of Nations – the forerunner of today's United Nations – was set up to provide an organization where countries could settle disputes by discussion rather than by fighting. Yet the League's effectiveness was always limited, above all because the US Congress, weary of foreign entanglements, refused to let the USA join. Without US backing the League looked too much like a European club – and one dominated by the war's victors at that.

Even so, the League marked a move towards a world in which reason rather than brute force would shape international relations. It set up the Permanent Court of International Justice in the Dutch city of The

Hague to try cases crossing national borders. Some people wanted to bring the kaiser and his generals to trial for such lethal innovations as the use of **poison gas** and unrestricted submarine warfare, as well as the invasion of **neutral** Belgium. However, the days when heads of state could be called to account for their actions were still in the future.

Losers and winners

Even leaving aside its terrible human cost, World War One effectively shattered the political ambitions of most of the nations that fought in it. The emperors of Germany and Austria-Hungary had sought to increase their own prestige and the status of their empires, only to come out of the struggle without their thrones and with their realms in ruins. Britain had fought to maintain its position as a **colonial** power, but in 1918 it found itself economically weakened and with its global position undermined. Its empire would in fact be gone within the next 50 years. France who had fought for security from her mighty German neighbour could take some comfort from winning back Alsace and Lorraine. But it emerged from the peace settlement to find Germany angry and still untamed and in a state to fight again just two decades later.

If World War One had any winner, it was the United States of America. The USA alone had the kind of war that the other powers had dreamed of back in 1914 – short and victorious. The nation had been on the rise industrially before that time, but the extra boost given to its economy by British and French demand for war supplies had brought boom times to its factories. The USA had demonstrated its military prowess and its industries now led the world. As for the European powers, they had gone to war to increase their own power and prestige at one another's expense. In fact they ended up paving the way for the American century.

Delegates gather for the opening session of the League of Nations in Geneva, Switzerland, in 1920. The League paved the way for today's United Nations.

43

Timeline

1871	German Empire proclaimed in the Palace of Versailles
	France loses Alsace and Lorraine to Germany after their defeat in the Franco-Prussian War
1872	League of the Three Emperors is formed between Germany, Russia and Austria-Hungary
1879	Germany and Austria-Hungary create the Dual Alliance
1882	Triple Alliance – Italy joins the German and Austria-Hungary alliance
1887	Reinsurance Treaty between Germany and Russia
1888	Wilhelm II becomes Germany's kaiser (emperor)
1890	Resignation of German chancellor, Otto von Bismarck
	Germany refuses to renew Reinsurance Treaty with Russia
1894	Franco-Russian alliance is signed
1897	Austria-Hungary and Russia agree to keeping the peace in the Balkans
1898	First German naval law, launching naval arms race with Britain
	Fashoda Incident sets Britain against France
1899	Britain goes to war with South Africa's Boers (to 1902)
1900	Second German naval law
1902	Anglo-Japanese alliance
1903	New, more nationalistic dynasty seizes power in Serbia
1904	Russo-Japanese War (to 1905)
	Entente Cordiale between France and Britain
1905	First Moroccan crisis pits France against Germany (to 1906)
1906	The Algerciras Conference
1907	HMS *Dreadnought* launched
1907	Anglo-Russian agreement signed
1908	Austria-Hungary annexes Bosnia and Hercegovina
1911	Second Moroccan crisis
	Italy goes to war with Turkey over Libya (to 1912)
1912	First Balkan War (to 1913)
1913	Second Balkan War
1914	Assassination of Archduke Franz Ferdinand in Sarajevo
	Outbreak of World War One
1915	Italy joins the war on the Allied side
	German U-boat blockade of Britain begins; *Lusitania* sunk
1916	Bulgaria joins the Central Powers; Romania joins the Allies
	Battle of the Somme

1917	Zimmerman telegram intercepted
	Russian Revolution. Tsar overthrown in March; Communists seize power in November
	USA enters war on Allied side
1918	Treaty of Brest–Litovsk signed between Germany and Russia
	US President Woodrow Wilson outlines his Fourteen Points for peace
	Germany signs the Armistice, bringing World War One to an end
1919	Treaty of Versailles
1920	League of Nations meets for the first time

Further reading

Reference books
Assassination in Sarajevo, Stewart Ross, Heinemann
 Library, 2001
Causes and Consequences of World War I, Stewart
 Ross, Evans, 1997
I was there: First World War, John D.Clare,
 Riverswift, 1994
The World Wars: Causes of the First World War,
 Stewart Ross, Hodder–Wayland, 2002

Novels and Poems
All Quiet on the Western Front, Erich Maria
 Remarque, Vintage, 1996
Under Fire, Henri Barbusse, Classic Books, 2001
Up the Line to Death: The War Poets 1914–18. Ed.
 Brian Gardner, Isis, 1997
War Games, Michael Foreman, Pavilion Books Ltd,
 1993

Websites
Website of the Imperial War Museum, London:
 www.iwm.org.uk

Glossary

alliance link between countries who wish to support one another

allies countries that support one another during peacetime and sometimes during war. During World War One the 'Allies' included Britain, France, Russia, USA, Italy and others.

annexation taking control of another country or territory

aristocracy people of high social rank whose position in society is usually inherited from their parents

armistice truce ending fighting

assassination murder for political ends

balance of power political doctrine aimed at ensuring no one nation is strong enough to dominate its neighbours

Balkans mountain range giving its name to a large region of south-eastern Europe

blockade use of warships to stop vessels entering an enemy's ports

Boer War South Africans mostly of Dutch or German descent (Boers), who fought a war against the British (1899–1902)

cabinet group of chief ministers chosen to decide government policy

casualties people who are killed or wounded

Central Powers Germany and Austria-Hungary

colonial describing the policy of the more powerful countries to take control of weaker or less developed parts of the world

communist someone who believes in communism, a political system where the state controls property, industry and trade

conscription compulsory service in the armed forces

convoy a group of ships sailing together and protected by a warship called a 'destroyer'

Crimean War war fought from 1853 to 1856 between Russia on one side and Britain, France and Turkey on the other

democracy political system where the government of a country is elected by its people

diplomacy discussions with other countries that are intended to promote friendly relations

disarmament the agreed reduction in stockpiles of weapons

Dreadnoughts heavily-armed battleships introduced in 1906

dynasty succession of rulers coming from the same family

Entente Cordiale the informal alliance linking Britain and France after 1904

foreign policy government policy concerning its relations with other countries

Franco-Prussian War a war setting France against Germany in 1870–71

free trade to be able to trade with any country without paying customs or duty charges

hierarchy ranking people one above another according to the power of their position

illiterate being unable to read or write

imperial to do with an empire and its rulers

industrialization the policy of encouraging the development of heavy industry

Industrial Revolution movement in the 18th and 19th centuries that turned first Britain and then other powers into industrial nations

labour unions organizations set up to promote the rights of the working people

merchant shipping ships carrying trade goods

mobilization the calling up of soldiers to go to war

nationalism belief that people's first loyalty is to their own national group

nation-state country where all the inhabitants speak the same language and share the same customs and past history

Nazism the extreme political views of the National Socialist Party in Germany during Hitler's time

neutral not involved in a conflict

no-man's-land wasteland between opposing

Index

lines of trenches in World War One

Ottoman the dynasty of sultans ruling Turkey and its empire from 1280 to 1924

patriotism love and loyalty for one's country

poison gas lethal gas used as a weapon

principality small state ruled by a prince rather than a king

protectorate country under the official protection of another country

raked refers to the sweeping movement used by soldiers using machine-guns

raw materials naturally occurring materials such as iron ore which can be used by industry to manufacture products

Reinsurance Treaty secret treaty signed in 1887 in which Germany and Russia promised not to go to war with each other

reparations payments from a losing power to a victor to cover the costs of a war

republicanism a belief in having an elected president as head of a country rather than an unelected monarch

Slav member of any of the East European peoples speaking Slavonic languages, including Russians, Serbs, Bosnians and others

sphere of influence countries or territories that other countries feel they have a right to interfere with

stalemate term (originally from chess) for a situation in which neither side can win

sultan Muslim ruler

theatre of war area of land where fighting is taking place

Third Republic the system of government in France from 1870 to 1940

Triple Alliance an alliance concluded secretly between Germany, Austria-Hungary and Italy in 1882

tsar the emperor of Russia

U-boat German submarine

ultimatum final warning threatening war

war debt debts run up in the course of fighting a war